500
WAYS TO MAKE Me
LAUGH
UNTIL I
explode!

500

WAYS TO MAKE ME

LAUGH

UNTIL I

explode!

Ticktock

An Hachette UK Company

www.hachette.co.uk

First published in the USA in 2014 by Ticktock,
an imprint of Octopus Publishing Group Ltd
Endeavour House
189 Shaftesbury Avenue
London
WC2H 8JY

www.octopusbooks.co.uk
www.octopusbooksusa.com
www.ticktockbooks.com

Distributed in the US by
Hachette Book Group USA
237 Park Avenue
New York, NY 10017, USA

Distributed in Canada by
Canadian Manda Group
165 Dufferin Street
Toronto, Ontario, Canada M6K 3H6

ISBN 978 1 78325 083 7

Printed and bound by CPI Group (UK) Ltd, Croydon, CR0 4YY

10 9 8 7 6 5 4 3 2 1

Text, illustration, and design: Duck Egg Blue
Project Editor: Mariangela Palazzi-Williams
Publisher: Samantha Sweeney
Managing Editor: Karen Rigden
Production Controller: Sarah Connelly
US Editor: Jennifer Dixon

Contents

Classroom Capers	6
Fun and Games	24
Animal Antics	34
Stop Bugging Me!	47
Crazy Folk	58
Funny Food	75
It's a Wacky World	88
Getting Around	99
Technological Tomfoolery	109
Doctor, Doctor!	116
Ghosts, Ghouls, and Freaky Fools	127
Out of this World!	136

Classroom Capers

Dad: How do you like going to school, son?

Boy: Going to school is fine. Coming home from school is also fine. It's the bit in the middle that I don't like!

Why did Betty eat her homework?

Her teacher said it was a piece of cake!

How did the music teacher get locked in the classroom?

His keys were inside the piano!

THE END

Teacher: Billy, how many teachers work at this school?

Billy: Only about a quarter of them, sir!

Hurry up! You'll be late for school.

What's the rush? It's open until three thirty!

Teacher: If I had six apples in one hand and seven apples in the other, what would I have?

Student: Big hands, sir!

What's the difference between a book and a teacher?

You can shut a book up!

Why is a teacher like a hiker?

They both ramble on!

Why did the teacher take a ruler to bed?

Because he wanted to see how long he slept!

Why did the teacher call both of her sons Edward?

Because two Eds are better than one!

How do you get straight As?

By using a ruler!

What did you learn in school today?

Not enough. I have to go back tomorrow!

Which object is king of the classroom?

The ruler!

What do elves learn in school?

The elf-abet!

Why didn't the nose want to go to school?

He was tired of getting picked on!

THE E

How does the teacher keep her class on its toes?

She puts thumb tacks on their chairs!

Why did the teacher wear glasses?

To control her pupils!

I don't think I deserved zero on this test!

I agree, but that's the lowest mark I could give you!

Teacher: What's the capital of Denmark?

Student: Er, "D"?

Teacher: How many books have you read in your lifetime?

Student: I don't know, I'm not dead yet!

Teacher: You missed school yesterday, didn't you?

Student: Not really!

Teacher: Can you name two days that begin with a "t"?

Student: Today and tomorrow!

THE

12

Teacher: Who is your favorite author?

Student: Minnie Mouse.

Teacher: But Minnie Mouse never wrote any books!

Student: You got it!

Teacher: How many months have 28 days?

Student: All of them!

Teacher: That's an excellent essay for someone your age!

Student: Is it an excellent essay for someone my dad's age, too, miss?

Teacher: If 5 people each gave you $20, what would you get?

Student: A new bike!

What does an elf do after school?

Gnome-work!

Why did the music teacher need a ladder?

To reach the high notes!

Teacher: Freddie, where's your homework?

Freddie: The dog ate it.

Teacher: Now come on, Freddie. I've been a teacher for over twenty years. Do you really expect me to believe that?

Freddie: He did, miss, honestly! I had to mix it in with his food, but he ate it!

Where's the best place to have the school nurse's office?

Next to the cafeteria!

Teacher: Amelia, why are you the only person in class today?

Amelia: Because I didn't have school lunch yesterday!

What's the worst thing you'll find in the school cafeteria?

The food!

I'm reading a book about a world with no gravity. It's impossible to put down!

What do librarians take with them when they go fishing?

Bookworms!

Why was the book upset?

It was left on the shelf!

How is an English teacher like a judge?

They both give out sentences!

CLIFF TOP TRAGEDY
by Eileen Dover

All Hail the King!
by Neil Down

How Not to Be Late
by Justin Time

All About Reptiles
by Ali Gator

Italian Cooking
by Liz Annia

Falling Trees
by Tim Burr

I Win!
by U. Lose

Bubbles in the Bathtub
by Ivor Windybottom

THE HOT DOG
by Frank Furter

Seabirds
by Al Batross

Parachuting
by Hugo First

Pull With All You've Got!
by Eve Ho

What's the first thing a king or queen does when they take to the throne?

They sit down!

8×9
11×6
4×2

What do you get if you add 743 to 288, then divide your answer by 12?

A headache!

Is a hammer good for math?

No, you need multipliers!

Science teacher: what is the center of gravity?

Student: "V"!

Why did closing her eyes remind the teacher of her classroom?

Because there were no pupils to see!

Science teacher: Stuart, can you tell me how fast light travels?

Stuart: I don't know, but it gets to my house very early each morning!

Where are most monarchs crowned?

On the head!

What did one math book say to the other?

Boy, have I got problems!

END-OF-YEAR SCHOOL REPORT

Student: Des Respectful

Subject: English

Des is an excellent communicator.
He never shuts up!

Subject: Science

He should have a great knowledge of marine life
because all his grades are below C level.

Subject: Music

Des is a wonder child — I wonder if he ever
listens to a word I say.

Subject: French

All I can say is that the subject is foreign to him.

Subject: Math

Math tests aren't a problem for Des.
He has never attended one.

Where do pencils come from?

Pennsylvania!

Geography teacher: Marty, prove that the Earth is round.

Marty: But sir, I never said that it was!

I have an excellent geography teacher. He has abroad knowledge of his subject!

Why did the teacher write on the window?

Because she wanted the lesson to be very clear!

Did you hear about the math teacher who fainted in class?

Her students tried to bring her two!

Why did the teacher turn the lights on?

Because her class was so dim!

Which queen burped a lot?

Queen Hic-toria!

Excuse me!

Where do knights learn to fight?

At knight school!

When I grow up, I want to be a...

COMEDIAN
(Joe King)

POLICE OFFICER
(Laura Norder)

CATERER
(Sam Which)

BARBER
(Sean Head)

GARDENER
(Rose Bush)

ACTRESS
(Holly Wood)

ARCHAEOLOGIST
(Dinah Soars)

MAKE-UP ARTIST
(Rosie Cheeks)

CONSTRUCTION WORKER
(Bill Derr)

Fun and Games

Why was the basketball court wet?

Because the players had dribbled on it!

Why did the stupid race car driver make ten pit stops?

He kept asking for directions!

I'd like to sign him up for basketball. I think he's going to be pretty tall.

Why can't elephants play soccer?

They have two left feet!

What is a ghost's favorite soccer position?

Ghoul keeper!

What goes in pink and comes out blue?

A swimmer in winter!

Why was Cinderella so bad at baseball?

She had a pumpkin for a coach and she ran away from the ball!

How is a baseball team similar to a pancake?

They both need a good batter!

What's a golfer's favorite letter?

Tee!

Michael's neighbor was walking up the drive, towards Michael's house. "Oh no," said Michael's dad. "The guy from next door is coming to ask to borrow something again. He only ever comes to see us when he wants something, but he won't get away with it this time. Watch this..." "Excuse me," said the neighbor, "Would you mind if I borrowed your ladder?" "I'm sorry," said Michael's dad, feeling smug, "I'll be using it all day." "Oh, in that case, " said the neighbor, "you won't be using your golf clubs. Do you mind if I borrow those instead?"

Why did the soccer ball quit?

He was tired of being pushed around!

What is the hardest part about parachuting?

The ground!

Why do penguins make good Formula 1 drivers?

Because they're always in pole position!

What do you do when you see an elephant with a basketball?

Get out of the way!

A long-distance runner runs
for three hours, but only
moves two feet. Why?

He only has two feet!

What's an athlete's favorite food?

Runner beans!

What animal is best at hitting a baseball?

A bat!

What race is never run?

A swimming race!

Did you hear about the nun who wanted to be a soccer player?

She was trying to kick the habit!

What did the baseball glove say to the baseball?

Catch you later!

Why was everyone so tired on April 1st?

They had just finished a March of 31 days!

What is harder to catch the further you run?

Your breath!

What is a runner's favorite subject in school?

Jog-raphy!

What should you do when the soccer field is flooded?

Bring on the subs!

Do you go rock climbing?

I would if I were boulder!

Why did the golfer pack an extra pair of pants?

In case he got a hole in one!

Don't dive, don't dive! There's no water in the pool!

That's OK. I can't swim anyway!

Prank #1

EASY ARM WRESTLE!

You will need: A mashed up bit of banana.

Place the banana in the palm of your hand and cup your fingers around it, so your victim can't see it.

Challenge your victim to an arm-wrestling competition and watch them get a shock as they grab your hand!

PRANK LIKE A PRO: You only need a small amount of banana in your hand for this prank to work. Use too much and your victim will probably spot it!

Simon: When I was climbing last year, I fell off a 30-foot cliff.

Mark: Oh my goodness! Were you hurt?

Simon: No, I'd only climbed 3 feet when I fell!

Why is a slow race car driver like a bowl of milk?

He keeps getting lapped!

What has 18 legs and catches flies?

A baseball team!

FOR SALE

PARACHUTE IN EXCELLENT CONDITION - NEVER OPENED

ONLY USED ONCE!

Animal Antics

Why did the monkey like the banana?

Because it had appeal!

What's an elephant's favorite vegetable?

Squash!

What is black and white and black and white and black and white?

A penguin falling down the stairs!

What do frogs order when they go to a restaurant?

French flies!

What kind of bird picks up heavy things?

A crane!

What did the peanut say to the elephant?

Nothing - peanuts can't talk!

Why do giraffes have such long necks?

Because they have smelly feet!

Why couldn't the two elephants go swimming together?

They only had one pair of trunks between them!

Why does a giraffe eat so little?

Because a little goes a long way!

Why did the forgetful elephant take up running?

To jog his memory!

What kind of key opens a banana?

A monkey!

Why does a flamingo hold up one of its legs?

Because if it held both of them up it would fall over!

Where do ducks keep their money?

In a riverbank!

Why do seagulls fly over the sea?

Because if they flew over the bay, they'd be baygulls!

What do you call a monkey with a banana in each ear?

Anything you like, it can't hear you!

That? A bird flying upside down!

What was the bird doing in the library?

It was looking for bookworms!

What's the difference between a fly and a bird?

A bird can fly but a fly can't bird!

What's a frog's favorite game?

Leapfrog!

What do you call a funny chicken?

A comedi-hen!

What do you give a sick bird?

Tweetment!

I can't remember my homing pigeon's name, but I'm sure it'll come back to me.

Which birds steal soap from the bath?

Robber ducks!

What dog loves to take bubble baths?

A shampoodle!

What does a cat like to read in the morning?

The mewspaper!

Michael and his friends were boasting about their cats. "I taught my cat to get my slippers," said Michael. "Well, I taught my cat to open the kitchen door," replied John. "You think that's impressive? Well, watch this video of my dog burying his bone," boasted Ralph. "What's so great about that?" laughed Michael and John. "My cat was filming it!" replied Ralph.

What's the most musical part of a fish?

Its scales!

What do you get from nervous cows?

Milkshakes!

What side of a chicken has the most feathers?

The outside!

Adam: I once got my dog to retrieve a stick from 20 miles away.

Luke: That's a bit far-fetched!

Give me my arm back!

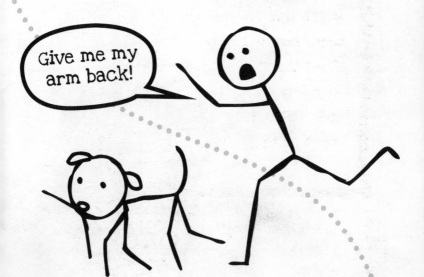

FAKE DOG POOP!

You will need: 4 tablespoons of peanut butter, 4 tablespoons of chocolate syrup, 1 tablespoon of flour, a little bit of sugar, a bowl, and a spoon.

Put the peanut butter in the bowl and mix in the chocolate syrup. The more syrup you add, the darker the poop will be.

Gradually add the flour until the mixture looks like cookie dough, then add a bit of sugar for texture.

Roll the mixture into log shapes and, hey presto, your fake dog poop is ready!

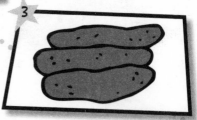

PRANK LIKE A PRO: This is sticky stuff so it's best not to use it on carpets, sofas, or beds – as tempting as it may be!

What do you call a rabbit with fleas?

Bugs Bunny!

Why wouldn't they let the butterfly into the dance?

Because it was a mothball!

What type of dog can you eat?

A hot dog!

A lady tried for years to teach her parrot to talk, with no luck. One day it squawked: "This cabbage is disgusting. It's full of bugs." "Wow! You can talk!" cried the lady. "Why haven't you said anything before?" "Well," replied the parrot, "I haven't had anything to complain about until now!"

43

Why do chickens lay eggs?

If they just dropped them, they'd break!

What dog keeps the best time?

A watch dog!

How do rabbits travel?

By hareplane!

What's a penguin's favorite lettuce?

Iceberg!

What do you call a sheep with no legs?

A cloud!

RIDDLE

A horse is tied to a rope. The rope is 6 feet long, and there's a bale of hay 15 feet away from the horse. The horse is able to eat the hay, yet it doesn't break the rope.
How is this possible?

The rope isn't tied to anything!

That Black Beauty - he's a dark horse!

What do you call a penguin on a tropical island?

Lost!

What do you call a grumpy cow?

Moo-dy!

What's a cat's favorite color?

Purr-ple!

Two goldfish are in a tank. One asks the other, "Do you know how to drive this thing?"

Stop bugging me!

Did you hear about the two bedbugs that met in a mattress? They got married in the spring!

What insect is best at telling the time?

A clock roach!

Where do rabbits go after their wedding?

On their bunnymoon!

tee-hee!

What's the biggest ant in the world?

An eleph-ant!

An Arctic Snail

What letter can hurt you if it gets too close?

"B" (bee)!

Where do you put an injured insect?

In an antbulance!

What do you call a 100-year-old ant?

Antique!

Why are mosquitoes religious?

They prey on you!

Where do wasps go on vacation?

Stingapore!

My life sucks.

Congratulations!

Two ants were running across the top of an unopened box of crackers. "Why are we running so fast?" one ant asked the other. "Can't you read?" was the reply. "It says to tear along the dotted line"!

Why don't anteaters get sick?

Because they're full of antibodies!

What's the definition of a slug?

A homeless snail!

What do you call two ants that run away to get married?

Ant-elopes!

Which insect runs away from everything?

A flea!

What's the strongest creature?

A snail – it carries its house on its back!

Which insect talks in code?

A morse-quito!

C'mon guys! The party's this way.

Picnic area

What did one flea say to the other flea?

"Shall we walk or take the dog?"

Why did the bee cross the road?

Bee-cause!

What do ants use to smell good?

Deodor-ant!

What do you call a Russian insect?

A Moscow-ito!

How do fleas travel?

They itch-hike!

Why do bees have sticky hair?

Because they use honeycombs!

Why did the fly fly?

Because the spider spied 'er!

How do you start an insect race?

One, two, flea - go!

Which insect can jump higher than a building?

Any insect - buildings can't jump!

How do you keep flies out of the kitchen?

Put a pile of manure in the living room!

What do you call a cheerful flea?

A hop-timist!

What do bees chew?

Bumble gum!

Why did the flea fail his exams?

He wasn't up to scratch!

Why did the mosquito go to the dentist?

To improve his bite!

Why do bees hum?

Because they don't know the words!

What did the dog say to the flea?

"Stop bugging me!"

Waiter, waiter! What's this fly doing in my soup?

It looks like the breaststroke, Sir!

SPIDER ATTACK!

You will need: Some thread, sticky tape, a few fake spiders, and a pair of scissors.

Attach a few small fake spiders to a length of thread and tape one end of the thread to the top of the door frame.

Close the door and fit the spiders into the space between the top of the door and the frame.

When your victim opens the door, the spiders will fall down.

PRANK LIKE A PRO: Don't forget to keep your camera handy!

SPIDERMAN!

What goes ninety-nine bonk?

A centipede with a wooden leg!

Why did the spider buy a car?

She wanted to go for a spin!

I must admit I'm not a great dancer. I've got 200 left feet!

Crazy Folk

Liam: If someone's brain stops working, will they die?

Kate: You're still alive, aren't you?

Laura: Why don't you take your little brother to the zoo?

Dean: If they really want him, they can come and get him!

My sister has lovely long brown hair all down her back - pity it's not all on her head!

Every night, William watched his big sister put cream on her face before going to bed. "What is that for?" he asked one evening. "To make me beautiful," replied his sister, smiling. "Well. It doesn't work, does it?"

Susie had just passed her driving test. When she got home after driving on her own for the first time, her mother said, "Oh, thank goodness you're home safe. I just heard on the radio that there was a crazy motorist driving the wrong way on the highway." "What do you mean one crazy motorist?" replied Susie. "There were hundreds of them!"

beep! beep! beep! beep!

What did the little boy's mom say when he asked her to buy some shoes for gym?

"Tell Jim to buy his own shoes!"

Max: Mom, there's a man at the door collecting money for the new public swimming pool.

Mom: Give him a glass of water!

CONFETTI UMBRELLA!

You will need: A box of confetti (or lots of paper circles from a hole punch) and your victim's umbrella.

While your victim isn't around, open the umbrella and rest it on the floor.

Empty the box of confetti or paper circles into the umbrella. Carefully close it and clear up any bits of confetti or paper that have escaped.

Put the umbrella back where you found it and wait for a rainy day!

PRANK LIKE A PRO: Help clear up after your victim has opened the umbrella. It's only fair!

Mom: The lady next door has a new baby.

Girl: What will she do with the old one?

Who is bigger - Mr. Bigger, Mrs. Bigger, or their baby?

Their baby, of course. He is a little Bigger!

A little girl and her mom are guests at a wedding.

"And who are you going to marry when you're older, Charlotte?" asks a guest.

"The boy next door."

"That's very sweet! Do you really like him?"

"No, not really, but I'm not allowed to cross the road."

Janet: Mom, do you know what I'm going to give you for your birthday?

Mom: No, dear. What?

Janet: A lovely teapot.

Mom: But I've already got a lovely teapot.

Janet: Er, no you don't. I've just dropped it!

Jonny: I was on the TV today!

Benny: You're kidding! How long for?

Jonny: Oh, not long. When my mom saw me, she told me to get off!

Whatever you do, don't stand on that! Whenever my mom steps on it, she screams!

63

IN A LATHER! (OR NOT)

You will need: A shampoo bottle with a top that screws on and a spout that you press down or lift to open, a small piece of plastic wrap, and scissors.

Unscrew the top of the shampoo bottle and cut a small circle of plastic wrap, big enough to place over the opening (about an inch).

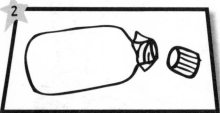

Place the plastic wrap over the opening and carefully screw the top back on.

Wait until your victim next takes a shower. Remember, they may take a while as they figure out why they can't get the shampoo out, so make sure you've used the bathroom first!

PRANK LIKE A PRO: Do this to all the bottles in the shower to really confuse your victim!

Scarlett: My gran's teeth are like the stars.

Molly: White and sparkling?

Scarlett: No, they come out at night!

"Dad, I've got a great idea to save you some money."

"What's that, son?"

"Buy me a bike, and I won't wear my shoes out so quickly!"

Alex: Dad, can you do my math homework for me?

Dad: I don't think it would be right.

Alex: True, but you could at least try.

What's old and wrinkled and belongs to grandma?

Grandpa!

Isn't it incredible? Nowadays you can telephone from an airplane!

Er, I've always been able to tell a phone from an airplane!

What do you call...

What do you call a girl with a frog on her head?

Lily!

What do you call a boy with a seagull on his head?

Cliff!

What do you call a boy with a pile of leaves on his head?

Russell!

What do you call a girl with an oyster on her head?

Pearl!

What do you call a boy with an insect on his head?

Anton!

What do you get when you cross a pie and a rat?

Pie rat!

What do you call a man who steals cattle?

A beefburglar!

Why are pirates called pirates?

They just arrrrr!

Where did the butcher go to dance?

The meatball!

Why was the musician arrested?

He got in treble!

Why did the pirate's phone go beep, beep, beep?

Because he left it off the hook!

Why don't cannibals eat clowns?

They taste funny!

Did you hear about the human cannonball?

He got fired!

What happened when the magician got angry?

He pulled his hare out!

A dog went into the unemployment office, walked up to the counter, and said, "I need a job." "Wow," said the assistant, "a talking dog! Well, I'm sure we could get you a job at the circus." "The circus?" asked the dog. "What would the circus want with a brain surgeon?"

Why did the baker stop making doughnuts?

She was bored with the hole business!

What did the criminal get for stealing a calendar?

Twelve months!

What are pirates afraid of?

The darrrrrrrrk!

Why couldn't the pirate play cards?

Because he was standing on the deck!

Why did the escaped prisoner saw the legs off his bed?

He wanted to lie low!

I've just had my watch stolen from under my nose!

That's a strange place to wear it!

71

Shop manager to shop assistant: You shouldn't argue with a customer. Please remember that the customer is always right. What were you arguing about, anyway?

Shop assistant: He said that you're an idiot.

POLICE – DO NOT CROSS

At the scene of a robbery, a policeman ran up to the inspector in charge and said, "I'm really sorry, sir, but he got away." "What do you mean he got away!" exclaimed the inspector. "I asked you to close off all the exits." "Yes, sir," said the policeman, "but he left through the entrance."

Did you hear about the demolition man's son who wanted to grow up to be like his dad?

He started blowing up balloons!

Customer: I'd like to buy a violin, please.

Shop assistant: Would you like a bow as well?

Customer: No. Don't bother wrapping it.

How do you join the police?

Handcuff them together!

Why are pirates great singers?

They can hit the high Cs!

"Why do you want to work in a bank, Freddie?"

"Because there's money in it!"

I used to be indecisive. Now I'm not so sure!

A man was walking his dog in the park when he saw two workmen. One was digging up holes and the other was filling them back in again. The dog walker's curiosity got the better of him. "Why do you keep digging holes and then filling them back in?" he asked. "Because," came the reply, "we usually work with another guy who plants trees, but he's off sick today!"

Quicksand!

Funny Food

What car does a farmer drive?

A corn-vertible!

Why shouldn't you share a secret on a farm?

Because the potatoes have eyes and the corn has ears!

Why do burgers feel sad at barbecues?

Because they meet their old flames!

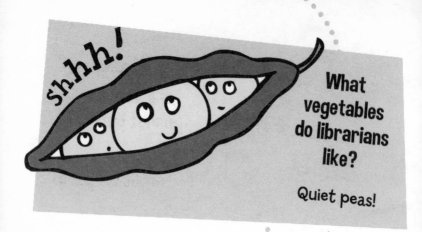

What vegetables do librarians like?

Quiet peas!

What happened when the rutabaga died?

There was a huge turnip at his funeral!

What's orange and sounds like a parrot?

A carrot!

What day do potatoes hate the most?

Fry-day!

What do you call cheese that's someone else's?

Nacho cheese!

Did you hear the joke about the peanut butter?

I'm not telling you. You might spread it!

What did the mommy tomato say to the baby tomato?

Catch up!

Why did the tomato turn red?

Because it saw the salad dressing!

What's a scarecrow's favorite fruit?

Straw-berries!

Why did the canteloupe jump into the lake?

It wanted to be a watermelon!

Knock, Knock!
Who's there?
Banana.
Banana who?

Knock, Knock!
Who's there?
Banana.
Banana who?

Knock, Knock!
Who's there?
Banana.
Banana who?

Knock, Knock!
Who's there?
Orange.
Orange who?
Orange you glad I didn't say "banana"?

BONKERS BANANAS!

You will need: A ripe (but not over-ripe) banana and a wooden toothpick.

Carefully push the toothpick into one of the banana's seams, about an inch from the top.

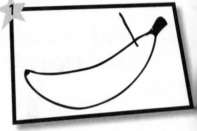

Wiggle the toothpick left and right inside the banana, cutting through the fruit but not the peel.

Repeat this about 5 or 6 times along the length to create a banana that will already be cut into slices when it's peeled!

PRANK LIKE A PRO: When offering it to a friend, you could tell her a story about how bananas are now being grown ready sliced!

What is a pizza's favorite relative?

Aunt chovy!

Why are hamburgers better than hot dogs?

Because hot dogs are the wurst!

Knock, knock!
Who's there?
Cash.
Cash who?
I knew you were a nut!

How did the farmer mend his clothes?

With cabbage patches!

Why did Mrs. Mushroom marry Mr. Mushroom?

Because he's such a fungi!

What did one egg say to the other egg?

You crack me up!

Knock, knock!
Who's there?
Beefst.
Beefst who?
Yes please, I'm starving!

What's green and sings?

Elvis Parsley!

Why did the wizard turn his friend into an egg?

He kept trying to poach his ideas!

"Waiter, waiter, how long will my sausage be?"

"About 4 inches, I expect."

"Waiter, waiter, my soup is full of toadstools!"

"Sorry, sir, but there wasn't mushroom for anything else!"

What can you never eat for breakfast?

Lunch and dinner!

Waiter, waiter, you've got your thumb in my soup.

It's OK, it's not hot!

A customer in a coffee shop was upset that the waiter hadn't given him a spoon. "This coffee," he said, "is far too hot to stir with my finger!" The waiter apologized, rushed back to the kitchen, and returned with another cup of coffee. "This one is slightly colder, sir," he beamed.

What did the angry customer at the Italian restaurant give the chef?

A pizza his mind!

Why didn't the hot dog star in the movies?

The rolls weren't good enough!

Knock, knock!
Who's there?
Doughnut.
Doughnut who?
Doughnut ask,
it's a secret!

Why did the clock in the restaurant run slow?

It always went back four seconds!

I thought you were trying to get in shape?

I am. The shape I've selected is a rectangle!

TOOTHPASTE COOKIES!

You will need: A package of cookies with a white filling, white toothpaste, and a flat knife (like a butter knife).

Twist the cookies apart and scrape the filling out with the knife.

Squirt a blob of toothpaste onto each bottom cookie and press the top cookie down until the filling is the right thickness.

Lay the cookies on a plate and offer them to your friends. The toothpaste will harden after a while, so make sure you can do the prank while it's still soft!

PRANK LIKE A PRO: Keep one cookie untouched and help yourself to it first before handing the rest out.

It's a wacky World

What's black and white and red all over?

A sunburned zebra!

Where do sheep go on vacation?

The Baaa-hamas!

What's the best day to go to the beach?

Sun-day!

Why did the turkey cross the road?

Because the chicken was on vacation!

See ya!

What do you call a cat on the beach at Christmas?

Sandy claws!

Where do worms go on vacation?

The Big Apple!

What lies on the bottom of the sea and shakes?

A nervous wreck!

What did the water say to the boat?

Nothing, it just waved!

Why is an island like the letter "t"?

It's in the middle of water!

What did the fish say when he swam into the wall?

Dam!

Who's that?

I don't know. But every year we sail past and he always goes crazy!

A flight attendant wheels his trolley down the aisle of the airplane. "Would you like some dinner, sir?" he asks one of the passengers. "What are my choices?" the man asks. "Yes or no," replies the attendant.

How do you cut the sea in two?

With a seasaw!

What do you find on small beaches?

Microwaves!

OOH, LOVELY NAILS!

You will need: Quick-drying nail polish (bright red or pink works well) and a sleeping victim.

Lay old towels under your victim's hands and feet to protect the sheet. If you manage to do this without waking them, then you're off to a good start!

Paint your victim's nails as quickly as possible. Always use a quick-drying polish - you don't know how long it will be before they move!

PRANK LIKE A PRO: This is a great prank to pull on an unsuspecting brother before you all go on vacation!

A tourist was trekking through the rain forest in Peru with a guide, when they came across an ancient temple. "Archaeologists are still excavating the site, looking for treasures," the guide said. "How old is the temple?" asked the tourist. "3,002 years old," the guide proudly announced. "Wow, that's very precise," exclaimed the tourist. "How come you have such an accurate figure?" "Well," replied the guide, "the archaeologists said it was 3,000 years old, and that was two years ago."

The Grand Canyon at night!

Why is the Amazon River so relaxed?

It just goes with the flow!

RIDDLE

What stays in the corner
but travels around
the world?

A stamp!

What is the smartest American state?

Alabama, because it
has four As and one B!

What is the fastest country in the world?

Rush-a!

Which city cheats at exams?

Peking!

If the red house is on the left and the blue house is on the right, where is the White House?

In Washington, D.C!

POP!

Teacher: Billy, where on this map is the United States?

Billy: Over there.

Teacher: Correct! Now, Susan, who discovered the United States?

Susan: Billy!

What's the most slippery country?

Greece!

I've just come back from a once-in-a-lifetime vacation. Never again!

Why did the girl study on the airplane?

Because she wanted a higher education!

STUCK FAST!

You will need: A coin and some glue.

This is a great prank to pull while you're sitting outside a café on vacation. Make sure you sit somewhere with a good view of the sidewalk!

When no one's looking, squeeze a bit of glue onto a coin and press it down hard on the sidewalk.

Wait for a minute or so while the glue dries, then head back to your seat and enjoy the prank in all its glory!

PRANK LIKE A PRO: Choose a coin of a value that your victim would think is worth picking up, but not so high that you won't be sad if you don't get it back!

POP!

What do you find in the middle of nowhere?

The letter "h"!

What do you call a boomerang that doesn't come back to you?

A stick!

Ava: How was your vacation in Switzerland? I bet the scenery was amazing.

Jenni: I couldn't really tell. The mountains kept getting in the way!

What's the coldest creature in the sea?

A blue whale!

I was away on vacation last week. It only rained twice, once for three days and once for four!

Which mountain is always on the go?

Mount Never-rest!

On the first day of his long-awaited skiing trip, a boy fell and broke his leg. "Why couldn't this have happened on my last day of skiing?" he sobbed as the doctor examined him. The doctor replied, "This IS your last day of skiing."

Why are mountain climbers curious?

They always want to take another peak!

Getting Around

A man phoned a cab company because his cab hadn't turned up. "My cab's not here and I have to be at the airport at eight o'clock!" "Don't worry," said the operator, "your cab will still get to the airport before your plane leaves." "I know it will," the man replied. "I'm the pilot!"

What did the car say to the gas pump?

Oil see you later!

What do you get if you cross a dog and an airplane?

A jet setter!

Who could hold up a bus with just one hand?

A policeman!

How many penguins does it take to fly an airplane?

None – penguins can't fly!

What's red and wobbles as it flies?

A jellocopter!

What has wheels and flies?

A garbage truck!

What's full of milk and has one horn?

A milk truck!

What do you get if you cross a broomstick with a motorbike?

A broom, broom, broom stick!

Why did the traffic light turn red?

You would, too, if someone saw you change!

Why do bicycles fall over?

Because they are two-tired!

Why did the farmer sleep under his tractor?

He wanted to get up oily!

Knock, knock!
Who's there?
Police.
Police who?
Police hurry up,
it's chilly
out here!

What happens when a frog's car breaks down?

It gets toad away!

Oh dear, I've just driven through a red light.

It's OK, dad. The police car behind us did exactly the same thing!

SORRY ABOUT THE DENT!

You will need: A pen, some paper, and your victim's car.

Write a note that says something like, "So sorry about the dent - I'll pay for the damage" and leave a fake name and phone number. Ask a grown-up to write the note for you if you think your handwriting might give it away.

Sorry about the dent! My number- 555-1234

Carefully place the note under your victim's windshield wiper before they return to their car, then watch as they try to find the "dent." So funny!

PRANK LIKE A PRO: To make it more believable, this prank is best done somewhere like a parking lot or busy street.

What did the tornado say to the sports car?

"Do you want to go for a spin?"

How do trains hear?

Through their engine-ears!

Jamie: What car has your dad got?

Jane: I can't remember, but I think it starts with "T".

Jamie: Really? Ours takes gas.

Why do hairdressers get to their destination quicker than other drivers?

They know all the shortcuts!

What do you get if you cross an electric eel and a sponge?

A shock absorber!

What only starts to work after it's been fired?

A rocket!

Check everything but the horn. That's the only thing that doesn't make a noise!

How often should you check for a puncture?

Every time there is a fork in the road!

What's worse than raining cats and dogs?

Hailing taxis!

Which driver doesn't have a license?

A screwdriver!

Knock, knock!
Who's there?
Cargo.
Cargo who?
Cargo "Beep, beep"!

106

Who earns a living by driving customers away?

A cab driver!

What happened when the blue ship crashed into the red ship?

The crew was marooned!

Two old ladies are on the train for the first time in years. They get their lunch out, and as one lady bites into her sandwich, the train enters a tunnel. "Have you taken a bite out of your sandwich yet?" she asks. "Not yet, no," her friend answers. "Well don't," the first lady says. "I just did, and I went blind."

Technological Tomfoolery

RIDDLE

You answer me, although I never ask you questions. What am I?

A telephone!

Where does an elephant carry his laptop?

In his trunk!

What do you get when you cross a computer and a lifeguard?

A screensaver!

REMOTE PRANK!

You will need: A remote control.

Sometimes the simple pranks are the best! Take the batteries out of the remote control, turn them around, and then put them back in.

Grr! Nothing's happening!

Put the remote control back in its usual place and simply wait for the victim to try and change the channel.

PRANK LIKE A PRO: Turning the batteries around instead of simply removing them makes sure that the remote control feels the same weight to your victim.

Sales assistant: Would you like to buy a secondhand laptop?

Customer: No, thank you. I can only type with one hand!

How does a cheerleader answer the phone?

H-E-L-L-O!

Customer: I cleaned my laptop and now it doesn't work.

Repairman: What did you clean it with?"

Customer: Soap and water.

Repairman: Soap and water? Don't you know you're not supposed to get your laptop wet?

Customer: I don't think the water was the problem, it's the spin cycle that caused the damage!

An unhappy customer went into a computer store. "Excuse me," he said to the assistant, "I bought a computer from you yesterday, and when I got it home, I found lots of twigs stuffed in the CD drive." "I'm sorry, sir," replied the assistant. "You'll have to speak to our branch manager about that."

What object has keys that open no locks, space but no room, and you can enter but not go in?

A computer keyboard!

Why was the computer cold?

It left its Windows open!

Why did the laptop keep sneezing?

It had a virus!

Mom: If you don't stop tapping away at that keyboard, I think I'll go crazy.

Harry: You already have. I stopped using the computer an hour ago!

tap tap tap tap tap tap tap

What did the spider do on the computer?

It made a Website!

What do you get if you type the alphabet ten times?

A sore finger!

Why did the computer squeak?

Because someone stepped on the mouse!

When doesn't a phone work underwater?

When it's wringing wet!

What did one keyboard say to the other?

Sorry, you're not my type!

What's a computer's first sign of old age?

Loss of memory!

Doctor, Doctor!

What do you give an elephant that's going to vomit?

Plenty of room!

Why did the cookie go to the hospital?

He was feeling really crumby!

"Doctor, doctor, I think I'm a needle."

"Yes, I can see your point!"

Did you hear about the man who lost his whole left side?

He is alright now!

"Doctor, doctor, I feel like a pony."

"Don't worry, you're just a little hoarse!"

"Doctor, doctor, I've got terrible wind."

"You're telling me!"

Mom: Doctor, my son has swallowed a coin!

Boy: But you told me it was for my lunch!

Doctor, doctor, Sometimes I feel like I'm invisible.

Who said that?

117

SNEEZY PEASY!

You will need: A bottle of water.

While walking with a friend, casually mention that you have a really nasty cold, coughing and sniffing as you chat.

While your friend's not looking, pour a bit of water into your hand. Then walk behind them and sneeze loudly while flicking the water from your hand onto the back of their neck. Gross!

PRANK LIKE A PRO: Practice makes perfect – this prank is all about timing!

What happened to the little girl who slept with her head under the pillow?

The fairies took all her teeth away!

Why did the pillow go to the doctor?

He was feeling all stuffed up!

"Doctor, doctor, I think I'm a bridge."

"What's come over you?"

"Two trucks, three cars, and a bus!"

"Doctor, doctor, I think I'm a cat."

"How long have you felt like this?"

"Since I was a kitten!"

Bob went to see his doctor to tell him that his leg kept talking to him. The doctor bent down and put his ear next to Bob's knee. "I need money!" said a tiny voice. The doctor knelt and listened near Bob's ankle. "I need money right now!" the voice said again. "Wow. This is serious," said the doctor. "Your leg is broke in two places!"

Why did the artist decide to become a dentist?

Because he was good at drawing teeth!

Ring Ring **Ring** Ring Ring

"Hello, doctor's office. Who's speaking please?"

"Er, you are!"

Patient: Doctor, I have a problem. I can't remember anything.

Doctor: How long have you had this problem?

Patient: What problem?

Patient: Doctor, it really hurts when I press here, and here, and here, and here, and here.

Doctor: I think you have a broken finger!

What did the tooth say to the dentist as he was leaving?

Fill me in when you get back!

Doctor: I've got bad news and really bad news... The bad news is that you've only got 24 hours to live.

Patient: And the really bad news?

Doctor: I meant to tell you yesterday!

Patient: Doctor, will I be able to play the piano after my operation?

Doctor: Yes, of course.

Patient: Great! I never could before!

Why did the clown go to the doctor?

Because he was feeling funny!

When does a doctor get mad?

When he runs out of patients!

122

What did one tonsil say to the other tonsil?

"I hear the doctor is taking us out tonight!"

How did the frog feel when he broke his leg?

Unhoppy!

"Doctor, doctor, I feel like I've been hit over the head with some maracas."

"You've probably got a slight percussion!"

Doctor, I've eaten something that disagrees with me.

No you haven't!

Patient: Doctor, I think I may need glasses.

Waiter: You certainly do. This is a restaurant!

"Doctor, doctor,
I keep thinking
I'm a dog."

"Sit on the couch and
we'll talk about it."

"But I'm not allowed
on the couch!"

"Doctor, doctor,
everyone keeps
ignoring me."

"Next!"

**What did the
dentist get for
an award?**

A little plaque!

125

What's the best time to go to the dentist?

Tooth hurty!

Why didn't the boy tell the doctor he'd eaten some glue?

His lips were sealed!

"Doctor, doctor, I feel like a pack of cards."

"I'll deal with you later!"

Why did the doctor tiptoe past the medicine cabinet?

She didn't want to wake up the sleeping pills!

"Doctor, doctor, I keep hearing a ringing sound."

"Answer the phone, then!"

Ghosts, Ghouls, and Freaky Fools

What's a ghost's favorite day of the week?

Moanday!

Why did little Dracula go to school?

So he could learn to count!

Why did the skeleton couple buy two cars?

They wanted a his and hearse!

What kind of horses do monsters like?

Nightmares!

Where does a vampire keep his savings?

At the blood bank!

What's big, scary, and has three wheels?

A monster riding a tricycle!

How do skeletons call their friends?

On the telebone!

It's much quicker, but I think it tastes better cooked in the cauldron!

Broomsticks are so last year!

What did the archaeologist say to the grave digger?

Show me the mummy!

Why did the skeleton cross the road?

To go to the body shop!

Why do ghosts fly?

To keep spirits high!

What's a monster's favorite game?

Hide-and-shriek!

What's white and red all over?

An embarrassed ghost!

Why don't mummies go on vacation?

They're afraid they will relax and unwind!

What's a skeleton's favorite musical instrument?

A trom-bone.

What did the monster give his headless girlfriend?

A neck-less!

What is a ghost's favorite kind of street?

A dead end!

How did the skeleton know it was going to rain?

He could feel it in his bones!

Why didn't the zombie go to school?

He felt rotten!

Why do witches fly on brooms?

Because vacuum cleaners are too heavy!

Why didn't the ghost want to dance?

He was dead on his feet!

What do you call a ghost with a bell?

A dead ringer!

What did the skeleton order for dinner?

Spareribs!

What do ghosts like for dessert?

I scream!

What's a mummy's favorite type of music?

Wrap!

What do witches put on their bagels?

Scream cheese!

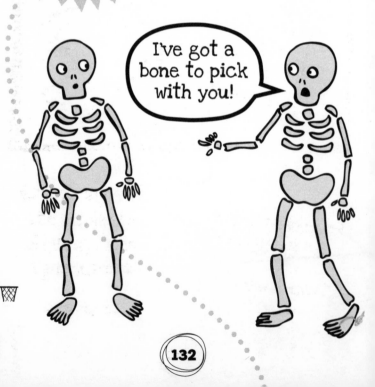

I've got a bone to pick with you!

What do you get if you cross a skeleton and a genie?

Wishbones!

Why did Frankenstein wreck his car?

He wanted new body parts!

How does a witch tell the time?

With a witch watch!

What do you call a skeleton who won't get up in the morning?

Lazybones!

Why didn't the witch wear a flat hat?

Because there was no point in it!

Why didn't the skeleton go to the party?

He had no body to go with!

Two boys were walking home from a Halloween party and decided to take a shortcut through the cemetery. Trembling with fear, they found an old man with a hammer and chisel chipping away at one of the headstones. The boys breathed a sigh of relief. "You scared us half to death. We thought you were a ghost! What are you doing working here so late at night?" they asked the old man. "Look at this," the old man grumbled, pointing to the headstone. "The stupid fools spelled my name wrong!"

FREAKY FINGER!

You will need: A small cardboard box with a lid (an old jewelry box works well), cotton balls, scissors, and some ketchup.

Ask an adult to help you cut a hole in the bottom of the box, towards one end. The hole needs to be big enough to fit either your index or middle finger through it.

Fill the area around the hole with cotton balls and add a few drops of ketchup to look like blood.

Poke your finger through the hole, put the lid back on, and go freak your friends out!

PRANK LIKE A PRO: For added creepiness, twitch your finger as your friend looks in the box!

Out of this World!

I spy with my little eye, something beginning with "S"!

What's the difference between a spaceship and a cookie?

You can't dunk a spaceship in your milk!

Two astronauts are sitting in a rocket. "Buckle up!" says the first astronaut, "it's almost time for launch." "Launch?" says the other astronaut. "But I haven't even had breakfast yet!"

How does the solar system hold up its pants?

With an asteroid belt!

Don't tell me you locked the keys in the spaceship?

Why didn't the sun go to college?

Because it already had a million degrees!

A flying saucer was running low on fuel so it stopped at a gas station on a deserted country road, much to the attendant's surprise. Along the side of the flying saucer were the letters UFO.

"Wow!" exclaimed the attendant. "Does that stand for Unidentified Flying Object?"

"No," replied the alien. "It stands for Unleaded Fuel Only."

What did the alien say to the garden?

"Take me to your weeder!"

What did one shooting star say to the other?

"Pleased to meteor!"

Why would nobody go to a restaurant on the moon?

Because there's no atmosphere!

What's a light-year?

It's the same as a regular year, but with fewer calories!

How can you tell if a planet is married?

It has a ring!

How do you organize a party in space?

You planet!

What sort of star is dangerous?

A shooting star!

What was the first animal in space?

The cow that jumped over the moon!

What's an astronaut's favorite music?

Rocket and roll!

What kind of plates do they use in space?

Flying saucers!

What kind of music do planets sing?

Neptunes!

What did the alien put on his toast?

Mars-malade!

What do you get if you cross Santa with a flying saucer?

A U-F-ho ho ho!

You were right. Humans DO exist!

FLYING SAUCES

How does the
man in the moon
cut his hair?

Eclipse it!

What did the
moon say
after dinner?

I'm full!

How do astronauts say they're sorry?

They Apollo-gize!

What are the slowest creatures in space?

Snail-iens!

What do planets like to read?

Comet books!

What's a spaceman's favorite chocolate?

A Milky Way!